WE ARE

Helpful "tools" in the Art of Reality Creation

Penny Snukst

BALBOA
PRESS

Copyright © 2013 Penny Snukst.

All rights reserved. No part of this book may be used or reproduced by any means, graphic, electronic, or mechanical, including photocopying, recording, taping or by any information storage retrieval system without the written permission of the publisher except in the case of brief quotations embodied in critical articles and reviews.

Balboa Press books may be ordered through booksellers or by contacting:

Balboa Press
A Division of Hay House
1663 Liberty Drive
Bloomington, IN 47403
www.balboapress.com
1-(877) 407-4847

Because of the dynamic nature of the Internet, any web addresses or links contained in this book may have changed since publication and may no longer be valid. The views expressed in this work are solely those of the author and do not necessarily reflect the views of the publisher, and the publisher hereby disclaims any responsibility for them.

The author of this book does not dispense medical advice or prescribe the use of any technique as a form of treatment for physical, emotional, or medical problems without the advice of a physician, either directly or indirectly. The intent of the author is only to offer information of a general nature to help you in your quest for emotional and spiritual well-being. In the event you use any of the information in this book for yourself, which is your constitutional right, the author and the publisher assume no responsibility for your actions.

Any people depicted in stock imagery provided by Thinkstock are models, and such images are being used for illustrative purposes only. Certain stock imagery © Thinkstock.

Printed in the United States of America.

ISBN: 978-1-4525-7556-8 (sc)
ISBN: 978-1-4525-7555-1 (e)

Balboa Press rev. date: 06/10/2013

I dedicate this book with love, to memory of my husband and parents, I also dedicate it to: my daughter, son, daughter-in-law, grand-daughters, all of the animals that have shared my life, and all of the people who have passed through my life, no matter how briefly. You have all made me who I am today; Thank-you.

Table of Contents

Introduction vii

Master Creators 1

Creating Process 7

Belief Systems 9

Like Things Attract 21

Synchronicities 29

Comfort Zone 33

Keeping Your Power 39

"Tools" 43

Pebbles in the Water 47

INTRODUCTION

I know I create my own reality. I know everyone creates their own reality.

It is one of those things I suspected my whole life, but was validated for me in the fall of 1972, when I first read a book called "Seth Speaks" by Jane Roberts. It answered my questions on things I thought were missing in my life and actually, life in general. But with that awesome revelation, I spent the ensuing years, studying the metaphysical, and learning how to do the creating.

I started this book during the holiday season of 1999, because my husband, Doug, and I, were excited about the "tools," we'd gathered in the creating process; we wanted to share them with others. This book, like everything else, is in a constant state of growth and change. Pinning it down and making it clear to other people has been the dilemma. When I first started, I printed out a copy of the "tools" and made a list of chapters and tried putting them in some kind of logical order. But each tool went into each chapter and the book got put on hold for one reason or another. At the same time, there were a lot of people waiting to see what I would write next because they'd been excited about what I'd already written. They wanted more information. Periodically, I would write a new chapter, but finishing it was a continual and changing process. Then in 2007, Doug passed away and finishing it didn't feel right, until now.

I have to explain a little about my life so you understand where my stories originate. I have lived in Chicago since Doug and I got married. During our almost forty years together, we owned a music store, where we taught music lessons, and sold musical instruments, we had a video production company, and performed every weekend in our own band. I still own the store, only now I just teach.

All of us are on uniquely different paths. You are all here to learn and grow from different experiences. It doesn't matter how close you are to someone, every person is on his or her own path. An example, if a problem needed to be solved, Doug and I would always arrive at the same conclusion, but arrive there from totally different directions.

Everyone has chosen the lessons you are here to learn. Everything you do, say, or think, affects everything else you do, say, or think, and not only does it affect you, it affects so many others also, like several pebbles in a pond.

All consciousness is connected and at the same time it's also multilayered and multidimensional. (I am going to be using those two terms very often in this book so here are some simple examples of each: multilayered is several things happening at the same time such as being a daughter, a sister, a wife, a mother, a grandmother, a business woman and a pianist all at the same time, and multidimensional is several things happening on different levels at the same time such as the mind, body, and spirit connection.) Again your life is so multilayered and multidimensional. You are not just the person you see as the reflection in the mirror. You are every facet of every person you have ever been or ever will be and you're being stretches beyond imagining in every direction connected to all consciousness. That is your reality. You are all master creators. Everything you have ever thought, said, or done, has brought you to this moment in time. It is the most powerful moment because you created it. You are your reality. Now with that mind boggling concept let's narrow the layers of your reality down to the one world that your brain can visually handle.

How do you consciously create your reality? Conscious creation is an art like playing the piano. For some people, playing the piano may come more easily than for others, but everyone can learn how to do it. You all know someone who has nothing but bad luck. He buys a new car and something is always wrong with it. He buys a house and it goes down in value. He goes outside and there's a sudden rainstorm. He gets all wet and then, a car driving by splashes him with water. He never wins at anything. He is looking for a new job but he can't find one. Then when he gets a lead on one, he arrives right after the position has been filled. He is always stuck in traffic, or always waiting in long lines.

You also know someone who is always lucky. He always wins at bingo or any other games of chance that he plays. He goes outside and finds money on the ground. He buys a new car and everything works perfectly. It runs for a long time and never causes any problems. He buys a house that goes up in value, or it is pointed out and pictured in a magazine. He goes for a new job and has no problem getting one. When he is out driving traffic always flows smoothly and he never has to wait in long lines. Everything goes right.

You are all master creators. Whether you like it or not it is true. Whether you believe it or not, it is true. You don't have to believe me. Just look around. God doesn't say, "Oh, I like this person so I'll give them all good things," or "I don't like that person so I will give them all miserable things." Like I said, look around. If you can't see it in your own life, look at your friends or family and see how they got in the position they are currently in. Most people are willing to accept, or at least think it's possible that you create the circumstances of your life, up to a certain point. When you have done something you perceive of as being good, or something you like, or of having value, you are quick to take the credit for it, and have an easier time accepting that it is possible, that you created it. But what if you are in a situation that you don't like or are experiencing something you are not proud of? Then you aren't so quick to accept the responsible for having created it. You say, "Why would I have done that to myself," or "I'd never do such a thing." But the fact remains that you've already created your life as it is currently. At the same time never berate yourself for the things you've created. You are a master and everything has a reason and is lessons and it is what you learn from these lessons that matters. But that also means if you don't like something, you can change it. As long as you are still alive in this life, you have the ability to alter your future; nothing is set in stone.

When I was younger, I searched for answers on how I actually create my reality. I wanted tangible answers. I wanted simple answers, straight forward answers, answers that made sense. Something like, wearing a special talisman, or surrounding myself with a special kind of incense, or at a certain time of day, face east, west, or whatever, or turn around however many times and this or that will happen. The more I searched for those kinds of answers; I learned they just weren't the answer. Instead, while other people were getting whole books written by channeled spirits, I kept getting the phrase, LOOK within yourself you already have the answer. What kind of answer was, look within yourself you already have the answer?

I felt much like the Peanuts' character Lucy, when she was talking to Linus and telling him that she had a lot of questions about life and she wanted answers. Linus answers, "Would true or false work?" Lucy's not happy with his answer and asks him the same question again. He answers, "five". Lucy is still not happy and takes her question to Charlie Brown. He gives her a list of all kinds of things like, eat right, avoid too much sun etc. Lucy is not happy with his answers either and takes her question to Schroeder. His answer is "Beethoven". The next frame, She has been told, the poets say, the answers are in the stars. She stands just looking up at the night sky, but doesn't get any answers. Finally she shouts, "Stupid poets," and walks off.

At the time, look within yourself you already have the answer,

was frustrating, and I felt much the way Lucy did when she shouted, "stupid poets." I wanted to shout "stupid answer," but I kept getting the same message, "Look within yourself you already have the answer is the answer."

You can't begin to know how frustrating that was. I was looking for tangible and what did I get, esoteric. Look within, I already have the answer. As my learning continued, I was amazed, when I realized, my answer, look within yourself, you already have the answer. It is the answer, and is also the answer for everyone. It has been an incredible journey.

I know I create my reality. The question was always how? I have some answers and hope that you enjoy trying them while you are reading this book. Enjoy.

Master Creators

Thinking about creating things has the tendency to conjure up wizards in long flowing robes, and tall triangular hats waving magic wands, but nothing could be further from the truth. You are all master creators. You have been creating everything in your life since before you were born. You are constantly creating whether you believe you do this or not. The creations happen whether you accept them or not.

You are all on your own paths; each reality is different. There is a purpose to everything you create. You have chosen the unique lessons you are here to learn. You can only create for yourself. The idea that you create your own reality, may have you are scratching your head and thinking, well I could have created the "good stuff," but this "bad stuff." No way! Why? How?

With the understanding, that you create your own reality, also comes the fact, that you have to take the responsibility, for you what you created. This is especially important when you want work with conscious creation and change the "bad" stuff.

All creation is from thought. You create both with your conscious mind and your subconscious mind. The conscious mind is the one you are aware of. It is the one you use to make your decisions. It is the one from which you say, "Think good thoughts and good things will happen." It is the one you use to do your positive reinforcement phrases and visualizations. It is also the one that reinforces your negative feedback. "I'm too fat," "I'm not smart enough," "I'm too smart," etc. It is also the part of the mind that lets you choose the outfit you are going to wear on any particular day, or what report you makes at school, or how you perform your job. It handles about 2,000 bits of information per second. That doesn't mean that every thought you have becomes a creation; most just fall by the wayside.

The subconscious mind is strictly habitual. Some 40,000 bits of information pass through your subconscious per second. It is what makes your heart beat, your lungs breathe, and does all the other bodily functions that you take for granted. It is also the place all of your beliefs are stored; the default systems. It strictly runs those programs.

Again, all creation comes from thought. All thought is neutral. Emotion and expectation are the switches that change the thought's strength or make it positive or negative.

One way of creating is with clear straight forward thinking. It is with a clear, focused mind. You think I want this and that's what happens. It's like placing an order in a restaurant and expecting the finished meal; done deal. It is making a statement and expecting results.

My son went to a Jesuit college. There was a priest there, who was always trying to exert his influence. When he'd see my son, he'd say something like, "You should stop by my office. We'll have a talk."

"I'm sorry Father, I can't. I have a class."

"Stop by my office after class."

"I'm sorry Father I can't. I have to work."

"I'd really like to talk to you."

"I'm sorry Father. I'm really busy right now."

I'd hear about these little confrontations, phone call after phone call, and I'd hear all the different ways he didn't want to get stuck talking to the priest. Their belief systems were really different, and my son, didn't want to upset the priest. He managed to avoid the priest for months, but one time he was working the entrance desk to a dorm. He was there by himself, studying, and he couldn't leave his position. Also he had no way of knowing, what was going on in the other parts of the building. Then in walked the priest, "So I never see you in church. Don't you believe in God?"

"Yes, I believe in God. I just believe things work differently than you do."

"How so?"

"I believe you create your own reality and what you think is what you get."

"Well that means if I say I want something, that it will appear right here, right now."

My son said, "Yes, as long as you really want it, and believe it will be here."

Then the priest, facetiously said, "I would like a piece of carrot cake."

The priest waited, nothing happened. He looked at my son and shrugged.

Then my son said, "You have to really believe it will be here. You have to taste it, smell it; make it real."

The priest, still humoring my son, made the necessary statements, in agreement. At that point one of the guys in the building came in and said, "We were having a party in class and we have a lot of carrot cake left over. Would you like a piece?" The priest never spoke to my son again.

When one young woman, who taught music lessons at the store, first started college, she still lived at home with her family. Sometimes it was easier for her to stay at a friend's house, which was a few blocks away from school. One of the days, while she was staying with her friend, she went in to take a shower. Her friend had a foot brush that was unusual. It was purple with a gold handle. She really liked it. She'd never seen one like it. She wanted one for herself. Then she forgot about it. The next time she was at home, and took a shower, on the bathroom counter was a foot brush that looked exactly like the one she had seen at her friend's house. Her mother had just bought it for her.

A young man, who taught lessons at the store, was on a trip with his family. They were talking about how things are created. He understands the concept and was tried explaining it to them. He said, "Make a statement."

His older brother said, "I want a dog."

"Are you sure?" he asks

"Yes, I want a dog."

They'd been driving out in the country, in a desolate area, with no one around. After driving a little longer, a dog darted in front of their car, and took them all by surprise. As soon as they recovered enough, the person driving pulled the car off the road. The young man I know hopped out of the car and went a little way back, calling the dog. It came to him. It was a black and white dog, young but not a puppy. He picked it up, brought it to the car, and handed it to his brother, "Here's your dog," he said.

Another way of creating is thinking plus emotion. Emotion and the intensity are triggers that set your creating in motion. They are the expectations, and practiced responses, that help create your reality. They are also the," I want this, but first that has to happens." You are usually unaware that you are doing anything, but it is your thought plus emotion. It doesn't matter which emotion. It is the emotion, and the intensity of the energy, you add to it that changes the thought from neutral; to positive or negative.

Usually, you think of emotion as negative, but I'm going to relate a quick positive emotion story. The first birthday I celebrated after Doug died, I had the most extraordinary birthday, because I created the most extraordinary birthday. All of my wishes were answered and more. It was a zero number birthday. When I had age and numbers mixed up, I would have been devastated, but that was long past. I was really excited about that birthday. I turned 60. My birthday, is near the end of May, and for me it meant my progressed sun, had moved into Leo, as I was born in zero degrees Gemini. It was the time for me to spread my wings and fly. I have been a caterpillar in a cocoon for so long. I celebrated that whole month. I learned some interesting things about myself, and brought many interesting things into my life. It seemed as if, I were getting a birthday present or more each day. Part of the celebration started in February, when one of my friends, who is close to my age said that she doesn't celebrate birthdays anymore instead re-celebrates the last birthday when she was happy, then she made a comment about my getting older. A young girl who worked in my store said, "Penny, isn't getting older she is going to be nineteen on 'our' birthday in March." Her nineteenth birthday, was that March. That was very sweet of her to say, and I had a lot of fun with her comment over the following few months.

One of the young men, who also worked for me, at the time, also turned nineteen that year. We shared a love for baseball. He is a Cub fan, while I am a White Sox fan; we have a fun rivalry. For a birthday present, he took me to a White Sox game. He gave me my choice, of the Sunday game right after my birthday, or I could wait until June for the White Sox/Cubs cross town game. I chose the Cross town game, but then one of our customers, gave us tickets to the White Sox game, the Sunday after my birthday. I got to see both games.

The day before my birthday, a friend who was working on my birthday, took me out to dinner. On my birthday, one of my aunts, who has the same birthday as I do; it was her eighty seventh. I thought it would be fun to take her out for breakfast on our birthday. When I arrived to take her out, my other aunt, and a couple of my cousins, joined the party. We had a good time. When I got back to the store, the two young people who were working got me a pizza and put candles on it. Then another of my friends, called and said she and her daughter were taking me out to dinner, not to argue. After dinner, they took me back to their house, where they had a birthday cake, presents and a birthday card, that played the song "Let the Sun Shine in".

Everyone went above and beyond making it a really special day for me. Then the following day, the store itself, gave me a present. I had been talking about training a new teacher, but hadn't done it yet. When an ex teacher, one of the better ones, wanted to come back to work here. That was great news. It was a fantastic birthday.

CREATING PROCESS

Most of your creating takes place and you are not even aware that you created anything, although you have created everything. Conscious creation of your reality is an art. Here are some guide lines.

1. You start with a thought.
2. Make a statement. Words bring reality. Always make statements in the present.
3. Expect what you want to happen. Believe it's a done deal.
4. Imagine what you want. Make it as clear as possible. See it. Smell it. Feel it. Taste it. Hear it.
5. Meditate on it for a small concentrated time each day. Visualize it as clear as possible. This is where you put up pictures, hang signs, use affirmations.
6. Release it into the universe.
7. Do something physical each day to reinforce what you want.
8. Say "Thank you."

It really is as simple as saying, "I want a piece of carrot cake and then getting a piece of carrot cake." It is that simple when you follow the easiest path when everything just falls into place and you trust it to happen. Done deal.

The next few chapters, show ways people have used some of the "tools", and what they created. Hopefully they will help you with your creating.

Belief Systems

A fundamental building block of conscious creation is you create what you believe. A belief acts as a filter through which you view life. Each person has a totally different belief system from anyone else, not unlike snowflakes or finger prints; all different.

A belief is anything you accept as a truth about your life. They can be things like: it is light in the day; it is dark at night, the month of February follows the month of January,

"I am fat," "I am thin," "I am pretty," "I am ugly," or anything else you hold as an accepted truth about yourself or of the world around you.

You have been forming your beliefs since before you were born. You chose the circumstances of your birth so you would be in the position to learn certain things from this life experience. So the kinds of experiences you learn from shape your rendition of reality. Then you gather things from what you see and hear around you. These experiences are stored in your mind as memories hidden away as possible programs in your subconscious mind to be pulled out and used by your conscious mind when faced with similar situations that arise in your life. Quantum theory describes them as the way the brain forms a network of neurons that fit together to find similar neurons that bring about similar responses. The more often those type of memories are called upon, the stronger the belief in the type of response, the stronger the belief.

Some beliefs that you hold, you believe, are created in stone and unchangeable, such as if you were raised with a specific religious belief, or how you view money, or how you view relationships. You look through those beliefs as what you expect the world to be like. Or you become "anti-those" beliefs because the world doesn't behave the way you think it should through those set of beliefs. There are beliefs you acquire from other people stating something that sound like it should be true, such as the commercial, "It's the flu and cold season."

My mother grew up during the 1920s and 1930s. There was still a heavy influence of prier nationality even though both my grandparents and my great-grandparents were born in this country. They were raised where their father was the head of the family; no question. Dinner had to be on the table when he got home from work; no exception. They believed the world religion was Catholic. I don't think my grandfather actually went to church but he sent the kids to catholic school. There were six kids in the family and even then you had to pay to send your kids to Catholic school. Their family couldn't afford it so they were asked to leave the school. My mother was very young at the time but that made a lasting impression on her. I'm not sure if she did all of the things required of growing up Catholic, but I do know as soon as she was old enough, she became a non-practicing Catholic.

My father wasn't raised with any particular religion. When they were married, they were married by a Catholic priest, not in church but outside the church because my father wasn't Catholic. Even though my mother was non-practicing Catholic, she was taught, and believed, you weren't really married unless the ceremony was performed by a priest.

My parents didn't attend any church but my mother thought that a good parent should make sure her child had a religious upbringing. She was anti-Catholic, and my father was anti-church, but, we had a neighbor who was big into the non-denominational form of Christian religion. She constantly gave my mother lectures on how I should get Christian upbringing, and because my mother was worried about raising me right, turned my religious training over to our neighbor.

Unlike my parents who never went to church, my neighbor went to Sunday school and church on Sundays and to a prayer meeting during the week. Also, they frequently had guests who were missionaries; interesting contrast.

Now all the while I was growing up, my parents said very little about my religious upbringing, except once in a while, my mother would mention that I could always become Catholic when I was older. So, I grew up believing that being a Catholic was something you did as a grown up. Also when I was a teenager, and still had religion and spiritually mixed up; I decided to be baptized into the religion I'd been raised in. My mother was horrified. When I was a baby, she had me baptized in a Catholic church. Remember, even though she was non-practicing, her early beliefs were that the only church was the Catholic Church. She gave me such a hard time and told me how I'd ruined everything. My father just said, "Are you happy with your decision?"

I said, "Yes."

He said, "OK." Nothing more was said on the subject.

That was the belief system of my early life.

Doug's family was all Catholic. He was raised Catholic. He went to a Catholic high school. His family was expecting him to marry a nice Catholic girl. When he brought me into their lives, they had problems handling the fact that I wasn't Catholic. And for a long time, they viewed me through those expectations.

My parents lived through the depression and were familiar with the lack of money. I was a little girl during the 1950s. We had a house in the suburbs that my father built. We were all right, but not rich. One year, my father received a bonus at work, instead of buying something they really wanted; they bought non-perishable food items. That made the most profound impression on me. It instilled in me the belief in lack of money. It made me believe, I had to make anything work, until even after it fell apart. I used little amounts of shampoo, perfume, or even certain kinds of food so I'd never run out. I hadn't realized how much that particular well hidden belief shaped my life.

Doug grew up in a household that believed you always bought new and always the best; bigger is better and two and three is always better than one. So, in our music store, he was always adding new merchandize, with never a thought how to pay for it. Neither one of us, actually had the idea of abundance in money down at the time, nor was our store account often overdrawn. First thing every morning, I'd run down to the bank to see which checks came through, and which I could cover. That was at a time the bank was still owned by a group of individuals, and not a large, unforgiving corporation. As my belief system changed, I learned to believe everything was covered, and my store bank account is now always in the plus column.

People grow up, wanting to believe, in your home you are in a loving, nurturing, environment, a safe place. I grew up in such a home. I was an only child and was often told, how much I was loved. My father and mother were my father and mother and only married to each other.

Doug's family was similar; his parents were his parents, only married once, and to each other. Both of us grew up believing that you lived in your parent's home until you grew up and got married.

The beliefs you hold shape what you allow in your reality. Most people become upset when asked to look within themselves and see, what makes them who they are. I have a sticker on my file cabinet that reads, "I Love Being Me." It took me awhile to be comfortable with that statement. I spent the past forty years studying my belief systems, and what to do to change the ones I have outgrown. I understand the process. I want to help you, understand your process, to help you understand how you have created what you've already created, and to help you create what you want. It is important to understand who you are. You need to know your realm, what makes up your life; know your beliefs.

To help you understand your beliefs, ask yourself these questions, really listen to your answers. If possible, write the answers in a journal. They aren't for anyone else, just you.:

>What is important to me? Why?
>What am I striving for? Why?
>What is positive in my life? Why?
>What is negative in my life? Why?
>Who is positive around me?
>Who is negative around me?
>What makes me Happy? Why?

What makes me sad? Why?
What makes me angry? Why?
What is my occupation? How do I feel about it?
What are my interests? Why?
What do I believe in? Why?
What do I constantly say that is positive?
What do I constantly say that is negative?
What do I constantly say?
Who is important to me? Why?
Who is not important to me? Why?
What am I doing to achieve what I want out of life?
What is stopping me from achieving what I want out of life?
What type of dilemmas do I attract?
How do I let them happen? Or how did I allow them to happen?
What are my thoughts for the future?
What are my thoughts for the past?
Who am I?
What choices have I made for myself? Why?
How do they affect my life?
What things do I like? Why?
What things I don't like? Why?
How do I feel about my name? Why?
How do I learn?
How does my thought process work?
What is my family like?
How do I feel about them?
What type of friends do I have?
What type of circumstances do I get involved with?
What type of obstacles and challenges are attracted to me?
How do I overcome these obstacles?

Here are some more examples of beliefs: I believe in my birthday. I celebrate my birthday. I celebrate, and I'm happy being me. Sometimes I celebrate my birthday, for my whole birthday month. It doesn't matter who else remembers, or what they think, I still celebrate my life.

Some of my friends believe in celebrating themselves on their birthdays. I know at least two who go on a vacation for their birthday. One believes her birthday is an adventure. She travels somewhere in the world she has never been. The other believes her birthday is private and doesn't tell anyone; but she goes on vacation then as a tribute to herself. Then I know someone who, believes her birthday is special, and to reward herself for being who she is, each year, she does something unique and that she has never done before. This past year she went sky diving. One of my cousins and her husband, believe their birthdays are a time of peace and togetherness. They get on his motorcycle and drive around the countryside, leaving all the normal day cares behind, enjoying who they are.

Then there are people who don't believe in celebrating themselves on their birthdays.

When I asked one I knew if was she doing something special for her birthday she said no, that she had stopped celebrating because her kids stopped giving her presents or honoring her in any special way; so she didn't believe there was anything to celebrate.

I recently heard two different radio show hosts say, they didn't believe their birthdays were special, and they never understood the fuss, or why anyone would congratulate them, or give them presents for turning a year older.

My husband, believed he had a bad memory, except when it was something important to him. He showed me that trait often, but most clearly right after we first met. It was our third year in college and we both had just transferred. We had a class together, (that's how we met.) and we went to buy books. Each of us encountered someone we had known from our previous schools. After his conversation, he looked at me and said, "Who was that?" He was surprised I remembered the person I had been speaking with. His defense for not resembling his "friend" was that he had a bad memory. With that in mind, he used to meet me after school, and my schedule was different every day; he never made a mistake. When I asked him about it he said, "You are important."

When I was a little girl, I had a neighbor who believed, he would live to be one-hundred, but no older. Every day, for years, in the summer I saw him out working in his garden, and in winter, shoveling snow. Then one day he wasn't out there anymore. His family said, he celebrated his hundredth birthday; then he simply stopped living.

The filter of beliefs does amazing things with how you create your life. One of the young men, who worked for us, believed everyone hated him. He saw the dark side in everything. The other people, who worked here, at the time, kept their distance from him. There is a pizza place a block from my store. When he went there for pizza, he would return with it, muttering that the people who worked at the pizza place hated him. "Whenever anyone else from here goes for pizza, their pizza is always perfect. They hate me. Whenever I go for pizza, and I get back, it is always all mixed up, and the pieces are on top of each other. They do that because they hate me. I should go back there, and yell at them. I should tell them how terrible they are, but that probably won't do any good, because they hate me." He always said the same thing. When he was like that, everyone stayed out of his way.

He believed the pizza people hated him, and deliberately messed with his pizza, but not with anyone else's. True, anyone else who worked here and brought back pizza, it was perfect. One day, after his pizza fiasco, he'd worked himself into a feverish pitch. He was so upset, he was going to storm right back down there, yell, scream, and demand, that they fix the problem. Then, with wide eyed innocence, another one of the teachers said, "Well if you didn't carry the pizza box like a suitcase, you wouldn't have that problem . . . DUH!"

The next story is the creation, of the sister, or of one of our students. The girl was sixteen years old. She was popular, and had lots of friends. She earned good grades in school. Then everything changed: she started drinking, her grades dropped, she got pregnant, but lost the baby. She believed she was so screwed up that in order to change her life, she needed something beyond herself, and really dramatic to happen. Then on a pleasant, late September evening, she attended a party with several of her friends. Before the party, she'd argued with her mother. They fought bitterly. Her mother didn't want her to go, but she insisted she didn't want to disappoint her friends; they were expecting her. In the end, she went to the party.

The party was in an apartment that faced a busy Chicago street. When the party broke up, fifteen girls spilled out of the apartment and into the night air. They were in a festive state. One of her friends lived halfway down the side street. She decided to walk her friend part way home. The two girls, separated from the group, and started walking. They walked as far as the alley, where she said good-bye to her friend. She way halfway off the curb, turning so she could head back, to the other kids, when a car, going around 70mph, came out of nowhere, and hit her It hit her so hard that she flung out of her shoes; she only stopped flying when her head hit a dumpster. The car sped down the street and disappeared into the night.

For several months, she hung between life and death. The doctors told her mother that her legs were so blown out that she would never walk again. Her vocal cords were severely damaged and she couldn't speak or swallow; with all of that, she slowly got better. A sports doctor was called in to re-evaluate the mess. He told her that with a lot of work, she should be able to walk again. The sports doctor started her on: physical therapy, how to balance, speech therapy, to help her learn how to swallow and speak, cognitive therapy, how to re-learn things like how to dress herself and how to wash her hair. Two weeks before Christmas that year, they pulled out the permanent feeding tubes and sent her home. At the time, she still couldn't: swallow well, get up to go to the bathroom, stand or balance. Her mother stayed with her night and day and worked with her continually. After six months she could feed herself and stand, but not for long because she still didn't have any balance. After a year, she could wash her hair, stand, and walk a little with the aid of braces. When we met the family, she was twenty-four. She could walk and talk, but still stayed at home most of the time. She still had no short term memory. She said she could think, but when she does, it made her work too hard and made her head hurt. If she wants to remember something she can, but if she doesn't think it's important to her, she won't remember it.

Her mother continued caring for her and continued to feel guilty for allowing her to go to that party. But she has an understanding of how her beliefs caused what happened. She asked her mother if she believed in God. Her mother said she didn't think so, with all that's happened, she didn't understand how God could let that happen. But the girl answered, "God had nothing to do with the accident." She believed she was so out of control and she needed a drastic change. If her mother hadn't let her go to that party, she believed the accident would have happened anyway. She was upset by the way she was letting her life go. She said to her mother, "Didn't you see the signs? It started with the throwing up, then the miscarriage, and then the drinking all of the time." She wanted to change her life and that she didn't think she could do it alone. She believed she needed something dramatic and life changing to happen. Getting hit by the car made her change her life.

The next story is my creation. I grew up in a Chicago suburb, about 23 miles west of the city. Growing up, I believed the city was full of scary things. That's what I'd been taught. I also believed in happy endings. I was a shy, scared young woman. When we first opened our music store and got married, the change for me was monumental. Our living arrangements were strange at best. We lived in the room behind our music store. When our daughter was born, we turned one of our teaching rooms into a room for her. One morning when she was a few months old, I woke up in the rocking chair by her crib; my German Shepherd puppy was asleep on my feet. We both, got up, checked on the baby, and headed back to our room. From the hallway, I could see into our store and out the front windows, into the street. As I turned to go in our room, movement outside caught my eye. I saw a white car. It drove past the west window moving very slowly. It was next to the curb moving west to east, when it got as far as the east window it took off at a high speed. I thought that was strange, epically since we'd had complications with broken store windows and some other things recently. When I got back our room I looked at the clock, which read 4:15 AM. I put the thought in my brain as strange, and went back to sleep. In the morning I forgot about it. The next night I was asleep in our bed and woke up suddenly, and looked at the clock. It was 4:15 AM.

I went to check on our daughter, when I opened the door outside the front window was the same white car I'd seen the day before. It pulled to the curb real slow, cruised past our west window, with purpose, got to the east window and sped off. That had my attention. I'm scared; two nights in a row, the same thing happened, at the same time. It is the middle of the night. Doug is asleep. What do I do? My first choice was to run quickly and wake him up. I decided against that for several good reasons. The main one being because at the time I was afraid of almost everything and saw danger everywhere, I didn't want to wake him up with some silly story. I went and sat on the rocking chair, with my trusty puppy by my feet. I figured I'd be good and not get hysterical. I'd just keep my eye on the situation. It was probably nothing, but my imagination. I said nothing. I just worried on my own. The next night I made it a point to be up at 4:15. In fact I was up a lot earlier and stayed up a lot later. I posted a watch and stood guard; nothing happened. I sighed, a huge sigh of relief! It was only my imagination; good thing I didn't tell Doug. The next night I was asleep on the rocking chair. I suddenly woke up. I went to the hallway. There was the same car, doing the same thing, at the same time. Panic! Still with my record of hysteria, I waited until Doug got up in the morning before I told him what I had been seeing. He was calm as he said, "Maybe they are just checking the store out. We'll keep an eye on it and see what happens." That night we were both standing watch, at 4:15, no car. We kept watching, about 5:30AM the white car pulled up to the curb in front our west window. Whoever was driving, performed the same ritual. They drove slowly past the west window and sped away when they got to the east window. That had Doug's attention. Why would someone be checking out our store, and at different times of the day; not a good sign. I was already a nervous wreck being in the city; this didn't help. While Doug was away the next day, I started hearing all kinds of sounds in the basement and the empty store next to ours. That night, when the same car showed up in the middle of the night and performed the same ritual, we decided we needed a plan to catch this dastardly person before he could do us harm. The plan was set: Sunday morning, Doug and another one of our friends would be in the empty store to the west of ours (That would place them where they could actually see the front of the car as it drove up to our building.), another friend would be in his car ready to follow the offending car, I would be in our hallway armed with several walkie-talkies (this happened long before cell phones) to relay messages between everyone.

When the day arrived, we took our daughter and dog out to my mother's house, returned to our store, and set our trap. Then we waited. At about 4:15 AM, our friend in the car sent the message that the white car had arrived. All three of them could see everything, while I could only see in front of our store. Walkie-talkie messages were flying back and forth: the white car had pulled up to the curb, it's moved very slowly, it stopped, the window was being rolled down, something was being thrown. The walkie-talkies chatter suddenly stopped; then I heard hysterical laughter. It was the newspaper delivery boy.

It is important that you understand your beliefs. They help you understand what you've created and how you created it. They help you create what you want. Remember that your life is created through your belief system, like a filter you put on a camera to slightly alter the color you are seeing through the lens; everything you experience will appear the way your beliefs allow.

Like Things Attract

Another fundamental building block of conscience creation is that like things attract.

Each thought you have has its own unique vibration. The type of thought vibrations you send out into the cosmos are the type creations you will get back. Like things are your destinies. You can look anywhere and see that this is true. Take a look at nature. Sand goes where sand is; a beach, the bottom of the ocean, deserts you see sand, not coal, or gold, or trees, you see sand. The same is true if you have gold, there will be only gold in the veins, not silver, or salt. In a silver deposit, there will be only silver, not gold, or coal, or trees. In a diamond mine, there will be only diamonds, not concrete, or salt. In an emerald mine, there are emeralds. And where there is water, there is water, like things.

Trees of a similar nature grow in groves and patches of similar type trees. Rubber trees only grow in the Far East. Tobacco only grows on the East Coast and in small patches in a few other states. Only certain areas grow blueberries or strawberries and areas for oranges and for grapefruits.

On individual trees all of the leaves on the tree are the same as each other. You don't have an oak leaf, elm leaf, and a pine branch all on the same tree. On an oak tree you have all oak branches, on an elm tree you have all elm branches, and on a pine tree you have all pine boughs with pine needles.

In the animal kingdom, when animals have their young, they are the same species: lions have lions, tigers have tigers, cats have cats, dogs have dogs, and birds have birds. Dogs don't have cats!

All animals search out the places that are best suited to their needs. Polar bears live in the north and are white so they blend in with the snow. Lions, tigers and other animals blend in with their environment so they can find food and stay safe.

The same is true for people. They gather with people of similar interests. An example is people with similar religious beliefs: Catholics will be with Catholics, Baptists with Baptists, Buddhist with Buddhist, and Hindus with Hindus, etc.

On a more personal level, the same thing is true of thoughts. There are people who are always lucky. Everything they touch "turn to gold." There are also people who are always unlucky. Everything they touch "falls apart." The difference between these two types of people is in the way they think. The people who think they are lucky are. Those are the like things they attract. The people who think they are unlucky are. Those are the like things they attract. They are both absolutely correct.

One Christmas, Doug and I helped two of our friends pick out their Christmas trees. The first friend we helped is one of those people that everything in their life goes right. At the first tree lot we tried, they had just gotten in a fresh load of trees. Her choices were of all fresh well-shaped trees. We only went to that one place. She got a beautiful tree and only paid $10. for it. She was excited and happy.

The other friend is someone who believes nothing goes right. She is a single mom with three kids who are unruly and unmanageable. She is always trying to get a job, but never does. She is the one who arrives right after a position is filled or gets a job; works for a few days and the person who just left the job reappears and wants the job back. She doesn't have extra money to spend, but wanted to give her kids a happy Christmas. We told her about all the trees at the place we took our other friend and about the $10 price. She waited a few days before she was ready to go for her tree. When we arrived at the store, there were almost no trees left. The ones they still had were bedraggled and looked like the "Charlie Brown" tree. She bemoaned the situation, now how was she going to get a nice tree and be able to afford it. We took her several places; they didn't have what she wanted. Finally, she found an acceptable tree. She spent over $45 for her tree.

A woman whose son was took music lessons at our store heard Doug and me telling someone else the person who is always lucky and the person who is always unlucky story. When we finished she said, she knew someone like that unlucky person that described her exactly. Everything in her life was going wrong. She had a job she absolutely hated. She needed to make more money because she wanted to send he son to a particular private high school, and she needed a new car. She was well qualified for the type of job she was looking for and had been sending out resumes for almost a year. So far, none of her effort had paid off. We explained how she needed to change her attitude and thoughts about getting a new job and see what happens. We also told her not to believe us, but to try the like things experiment for herself. The next week she came back all excited. She told us that she had gotten a new job. The job paid more money than the old one, she could send her son to the high school she wanted, and the new job had additional benefits. It was located across the street from her old job, so she could still park in same spot and still have lunch with her same friends. She was so excited that the experiment worked.

The things you think bring the like things you think. People who are focused on certain things will surely bring those things into their lives.

A young man, who was a teacher in the store, started seeing car accidents, when he was out driving his car. At first he saw the every few days, then, he would come to work and tell us about them; most were of a more major type, cars driving through fences, ambulances and police vehicles everywhere, those kinds of accidents. This started happening right after he learned the like things principle. Doug and I told him to watch out what you are bringing in your realm. He'd let out a deep sigh, as if to tell us, yeah right. Then he started seeing car accidents every time he was out driving, sometimes more than one. Then one day he was driving and not paying close attention; he rear-ended a car. It wasn't a serious accident, but for him, it was a serious wake-up call. He started thinking about what he had learned and why the car things. He tracked the thought back, to his focusing, on how his car had started costing him so much money. He figured he should rethink the whole thing, but the car accident reinforced his focus on his car. Then a few days later, when he stepped outside, no car; it had been stolen. The police weren't too encouraging about getting it back, so now what? He borrowed his parent's car. A few days later, while driving through the parking lot at the college he was attending, a car almost backed into him, but as he swerved to miss the car he drove into a wall. Now, instead of only worrying about his car, he also had the responsibility of fixing his parents' car. He went back to thinking about how he created the mess with the cars. He still wasn't sure about the like things, but since all of those "not good" things happened, he thought he would try switching his thinking to good things happening with cars. The first thing, he stopped seeing car accidents. Then he thought, "I'm going to get my car back." A few days after that, he got a call from the police and was told to come pick up his car. He decided that the whole car thing, was because he was focused on how much money the car was costing him; he got rid of the car. The next day, the mother of one of his students, told him that she had a terrible time because of her car. She had been in an accident and then it had gotten stolen. Then, she borrowed a family member's car and gotten in an accident. All he could say was, "Me too."

His car connection like things didn't stop there. He was intrigued with how he brought about his car disasters; he wanted to try playing around with his thoughts to see what he could create. This time he thought it should be something fun, something where he or anyone else wouldn't get hurt, and only good would happen; he decided he wanted to see a Ferrari. The area around the store is definitely not a Ferrari area. He put the thought out. Then while driving to work a shiny black car whizzed past; the speed the car was traveling, only gave him time to make out the Ferrari label. A few days later he saw another black Ferrari. The following day he, and his brother, traveled forty miles out of the city to visit a friend. On the way back, he told his brother about the Ferrari thing. When they stopped at a red light, a red Ferrari pulled up next to them. He was so pleased seeing the Ferraris, he decided to try something different; a Lamborghini. He got similar results.

One year, Doug and I attended a wedding in Canada, both as friends of the groom and as their video company. At the time, there was a big problem with caterpillars, and consequently, moths; they were everywhere. The caterpillars were spindly and about an inch long. The wedding guest's main conversations were about the caterpillars and how hated them. The bride was epically freaked out by them. After the ceremony, we went to a park to take pictures—and yes, there were a lot of caterpillars hanging and crawling everywhere. Since Doug and I were doing the video, so we were out there, too. All of the people who were talking about how much they hated the critters drew them right to themselves. The bride's intense fear, like a magnet, drew them to her. There was an abundance dropping from the trees and landing on her dress and in her hair. She was screaming and jumping around. Her bridesmaids and anyone else around were pulling caterpillars off of her like crazy. The people who were focusing on the caterpillars had caterpillars to contend with, while the people who weren't having a problem weren't having a problem.

When I was in high school, I had an Art History teacher who hated the projector. We used it every day to show slides of the periods of art that we were studying. Each day, he would set up the projector and would have problems: it wouldn't plug it in the electric socket, it wouldn't turn on, it wouldn't focus, etc. Every day he had an issue, and every day he told us how much he hated the projector; but every day, it eventually worked. Although it wasn't our teacher's intention, the process entertained the whole class. What we found more entertaining, was that none of the other classes that used the slide projector, had problems with it. On the day of the final exam, the teacher set up the machine, carefully checked everything so it would work, and turned it on; nothing happened. Then without warning, the projector appeared to jump off the desk. When he picked it up, it was damaged beyond repair. The teacher was beside himself. Needless to say the exam was re-scheduled.

One young man who taught and studied guitar at our music store, went on a cruise with his parents. His focus was so much on music, that many of the young people sharing his common room also played instruments. At one point when he was going down a flight of stairs and wishing he had one of his guitars so he could practice. When he looked up, he saw a young man, around his age, carrying a guitar. They started talking, became friends, and he got to play the guitar. On that cruise, he also met and become friends with several musicians that worked on the ship.

I heard a really good story that illustrates how like things attract. There was a young woman who woke up one morning with a pimple on her nose. At her age, that was upsetting enough; the following day she was supposed to have her picture taken. At school, she bemoaned her problem to her friends; being good friends they assured her that she looked fine. One friend gave her some medication that should really "do the trick." She went home and diligently applied the medication. The next morning, she discovered that she had a reaction to the medication and the pimple looked much worse. She didn't want to go to school, and definitely didn't want her picture taken, but there was nothing she could do about it. When she got to school, she thought everyone was looking at her. Again, her friends her calmed down when someone came by and teasingly called her "Rudolf." That sent her went running down the hall in a panic. As she got to a closed door, someone was coming out, and she got hit really hard with the door. Now, not only did she have the pimple, she also had a bump on her head and two black eyes.

There were times in the music store, when a particular type of instrument, let's say a banjo, would hang on the wall for months, no one asked about it or anything dealing with banjos. Then, out of the blue, someone would call and ask about banjos, followed by someone who came in and bought a set of banjo strings, followed by someone else who bought a set of banjo strings, followed almost immediately by someone who bought the banjo.

There was something that was upsetting me a lot; I used the term, "really bugging me.". I didn't tell anyone what was bothering me or that I was upset, but I was annoyed. I went out of town for a few days. On one of the days, I was outside helping someone put a swing set together. I wasn't rolling around on the ground or even sitting on the ground, but when I went inside there was a black spot on my leg. I was really surprised. I pulled the black spot off and was dismayed to see that it had little wiggly legs. It was a tick. I had never even seen a tick before. I looked at in fascination and then got rid of it. I found four in total, when I realized the problem, I was avoiding, was literally bugging me. I knew exactly what was on my mind, and at the same time I had the solution; everything dealing with the problem cleared up.

As an introduction to the synchronicity chapter, there was an interesting synchronicity dealing with the tick story. While I was dealing with the ticks, Doug knew something was bothering me, because at the same time, his skin broke out in blotches. When I cleared the problem in my head, and the ticks were gone, the blotches also cleared from Doug's skin.

SYNCHRONICITIES

If like things are your destinies, synchronicities, are the clues. They appear as unrelated coincidences leading to your like things.

The like thing was energy healing. I first heard about and learned to do, a type of hands on energy healing, in the fall of 1971. I was very excited about being able to do that, but in 1971 that wasn't the thing you ran around announcing. I used what I leaned on family and friends. Then as with a lot of things, life has a way of getting in the way and I let that ability fade into the background,. Then near the end of 1999, random people would ask me if I was a healer, and when I told them no, they demanded to know why not. That did get me thinking about healing again though. At the time, being that I'm involved in music, I was checking into tuning fork healing. My husband was always up in the middle of the night and always listened to a radio program called "Coast to Coast." When they had on a show, I be particularly interested in he would tell me about it in the morning, and I'd listened to it on their web site. One night he heard and interview with Eric Pearl . . . Reconnective Healing. I listened to the program and knew I had to study with that man, and that brought me back to practicing energy healing. Another synchronistic addition to that story, my son lived in San Francisco then and when I looked up where Eric Pearl's next seminar was. It was in San Francisco.

Like I just mentioned my son lived in San Francisco. Near one of his birthdays, I made the statement, "I want to visit him for his birthday." At the time I made the statement, I had no money to travel, and no place to stay when I got there. There was a woman who took music lessons and practiced at the store, she overheard my comment. She worked for one of the airlines and offered to get me on her airline as family and she actually paid the small fare. At the same time she was offering me the way to get there, my son's girlfriend, e-mailed me and wanted to know if I could manage to get there to surprise him for his birthday. She'd pick me up at the airport, and I could stay with them. Needless to say I went.

One of our ex-students, who we hadn't seen in about six months, called unexpectedly, one day. She said there was no special reason for the call. She just called to say hello and see how we were doing. A week after that phone call, she stopped in the store. She spent the afternoon visiting; when she left, she had a new guitar. The interesting thing about that was her instrument of choice; it was the banjo. When she studied here, she had no interest in buying a guitar. She said though, that when she was in for one of her banjo lessons, Doug was playing different guitars for someone who was looking for a guitar. When she heard him play one particular guitar, she absolutely fell in love with its sound and wanted to own it. She then stated again that she has no interest in playing guitar and no reason for owing a one. Time went by, because of her job, she had to quit lessons. She said she still played banjo all of the time, but also owning the guitar she heard, stayed in her mind. She said, she even mentioned it to someone she at work. He told her, if it made her happy, she should get it for herself. Her excuse was that, she didn't have the money to waste on it. But when she received her monthly bank statement, there was more money than she expected. Now she had the money, but she still put off buying the guitar. When she called us to say hello, she never asked about it. She also didn't mention it again to her coworker, but when she left work on that Friday her coworker said, "Tell me all about your new guitar, on Monday." She told him, no that that wasn't going to happen, she wasn't even planning on coming to the store, and wasn't sure we still had it. But she did come to the store and bought the guitar.

Even before my last white German Shepherd dog, Blizzard, passed away, I was dreaming about a puppy. At that time, the two best German Shepherd dogs in the world were living with my husband and me; a puppy was the farthest thing from my mind, but I kept having periodic dreams about a white, female, German Shepherd, puppy, named Magic. The dreams faded, and months later, Blizzard passed away. We were concerned about our other dog, an older, black and tan, German Shepherd. She and Blizzard were very close, and we wanted another companion for her. That was a Mother's Day weekend, and we adopted Sasha, a black and tan, German Shepherd, from a rescue organization. She helped all of us adjust, to the loss of Blizzard. Then, around August, I started having puppy dreams again. The puppy looked the same as the other dreams, but her name was, Zoey. Then the dreams would alternate; Magic, then Zoey. Doug and I talked about getting another white German Shepherd, but first we wanted to give Sasha time to settle in, and become part of our family. Right near Christmas, we when were out having lunch, I pulled out a pet store ad, from the newspaper, and said, "It looks like it's time for a puppy." We weren't going to get a puppy from the pet store, but I had it on the on the counter in the store, when a friend of ours saw it. She was against pet store animals, and gave us a hard time, about the ad. I told her we weren't getting one from there, but it was time for a new puppy. The next day, she called and told us about a breeder in Indiana who had white German Shepherd puppies. She gave me the phone number. I called him and we went out there on Christmas Eve. We came home with not one, but two white German Shepherd puppies; Magic and Zoey.

 Synchronicities are everywhere. They are in everything you do, say, or, think. They are the clues that lead to your, like things.

COMFORT ZONE

Your comfort zone is the beliefs with which you are comfortable. That doesn't mean that you have to like those beliefs, it is simply the beliefs you are used to. It is somewhere within you, where you operate your life from, somewhere you feel safe with what you know and can deal with.

Creating from you comfort zone has to do with the way you let things into your life.

It is full of practiced responses and beliefs you are content with. If the things you are creating are part of your comfort zone, it is easy for you to let them into your life. If it is something that is not in your comfort zone, you have a difficult time, letting the new thing in your life. Change of any kind is often difficult for people because of how they think.

You create through the eyes with which you view the world. You create from your comfort zone, which are the things you let into your reality, your life, around you. That is why whenever you learn something new, it could be really beneficial that you try it out with great enthusiasm and try what you learned and then let it fall by the was side. Or you hear about something that could really help and you just ignore it. You go back to your comfort zone. That is why whenever you learn something new, that is really beneficial you try it out with great enthusiasm and try what you learned and then let it fall by the was side. Or you hear about something that could really help and you just ignore it. You are afraid and resistant to it until you can stretch your comfort zone to fit it in and make it part of your life. You let it in small amounts until the new thing is a practiced response stretching the boundaries of your comfort zone.

The next two stories are simple stories from what used to be my comfort zone, these both happened while my main concern was Doug, who was very sick. I just went to make myself a cup of tea. I like tea and I grew up drinking tea. Now I heard that having a ½ cup boiled water & ½ distilled mixed together was a better substitute, so I tried that for awhile I didn't see any dramatic changes or even changes at all. Then I also tried green tea with all of its benefits and I did that for almost a year, and I really like green tea, but one day, I decided I just wanted a cup of regular old tea; and that's what I had. For me, regular old tea is Lipton; I grew up with it and it's a comfort tea. So after the day, I've been drinking Lipton again. Since then, I've been introduced to designer loose leaf tea and I just plain hot water. I like them both; they have replaced the old way, so I've expanded that comfort zone.

Worrying about Doug had a lot to do with this comfort zone story. I've been sleeping on a living room chair, (over-sized chair that fits me and one German shepherd comfortably) for the years since Doug's first heart failure. Before then, we had a full motion water bed in our bedroom. Doug was ok with the water bed; I loved our water bed, it was a comfort zone for me. After his first heart failure, he was more comfortable sleeping on the living room couch. To make sure he was all right, I moved to the chair. My son was vigilant in telling me that I was grown up and that I should get rid of the water bed. After Doug and I moved to the living room, he disassembled the water bed. So after Doug died, I was used to sleeping on the chair. That was when my son decided I needed a bed. He was worried I wasn't getting any rest sleeping sitting or curled in my chair. I told him that I was perfectly happy; besides, usually one of the dogs would be cuddled up with me, and I liked that. He reminded me I didn't have to stand guard anymore and I needed better rest. I insisted I was fine and I liked the chair. It had become a comfort zone. I could read there easily, and since I read a lot, I didn't want the change. He got me an inflatable bed. The first night I ignored it. The second night I tried it. It was ok, but I woke up in the middle of the night, and went back to the chair. He lives in the San Francisco area, but would call and ask where I slept. Usually, I said on the chair. He'd give me a lecture on how it was better for me on the bed. This went on for several days, when I finally slept on the bed again, I could hear the sound of escaping air, and in the morning I felt like I was a lot closer to the ground. The dogs hadn't done anything to the bed, they hadn't been near it, and when it wasn't in use, it was in a room the dogs didn't have access to. So I got the pump and tried inflating it. The pump didn't work. The next time he called, I told him the bed had a problem and so did the pump. He told me to blow it up like a balloon. I asked someone else pump it up. I set the freshly pumped up bed safely in the room and left. When I came back, the bed was totally flat and clasped over on the floor. I called him, and said the bed was dead. He came up with more ways for me to fix it. I finally told him, no bed. He informed me we would figure the bed out when I went to visit him at Christmas, which was right about to happen.

The room I slept in when I visited my son had two beds and a chair similar to the one I have at home. The first night I read until I feel asleep in the chair. In the morning, he asked me where I slept. I told him in the chair. He wanted to know why when there two good beds right there that I didn't sleep in either bed. I told him I was reading and I couldn't get my head high enough to be comfortable and read. He told me to put some of the stuffed animals under my head and lectured me in being unwilling to accept change. I thought about what he said and realized the whole bed thing had to do with my comfort zone, and that most people are resistant to change of any kind when it affects their comfort zone. So, that night, I decided to sleep in the bed. I put stuffed animals under my head and tipped the lamp shade so I could read. I wasn't happy, and the next night, I slept in the chair. He said if I didn't sleep in the bed he would take the chair out of the room. By the last day I was there, I slept in the bed.

I used to own something that looked like a chair, but you could unfold it and would have a cushion about six inches off the ground. I thought that would be perfect. So while I was out in California, we looked on line and actually found what I wanted. I put my order in from there, and it was delivered to me in Chicago.

Back home, I had at least a week wait so I could sleep in my chair, with no one giving me a hard time. It was a Wednesday when the bed arrived. My neighbor's business that usually takes my packages was closed, so when it's time to open my store, I go downstairs and have two delivery notices. The bed was delivered by not my company of choice; it turned into a chaotic mess. By the time it actually arrived, I was laughing and having a great time because I understood the mess I created all because I didn't want the bed.

Even after the bed arrived, and was up stairs, it was waiting to be unwrapped. I forgot about it. I woke up from my chair in the middle of the night and remembered I hadn't even opened the package. And I wasn't going to open it in the middle of the night because I would have to turn the light on in the bedroom and I didn't want to disturb my birds. The next morning I finally got the bed set up. It has been set up since then and I sleep on it once in awhile.

One short post script to this whole story, I hadn't wanted my sleeping arrangements changed and was very resistant to the change, especially in the beginning. The dead, inflatable mattress had found a home on the floor on the opposite side of my bedroom from my new "bed." It stayed like that for a couple of weeks, when in the middle of one night, all four of my dogs were up romping around in my room when my oldest one decided to pee on the inflatable bed. A perfect ending to what I thought of the whole idea.

The woman, who was a neighbor, was a real live soap opera. Every day, she had a new complication in her life, or more correctly the same complication with a new twist. She hated her apartment and she hated her landlord. She was a waitress, she liked being a waitress, but hated her job, and she hated her boss. She had her three kids (these aren't babies, one was 20 one 19 and one 17) and her year old grand-daughter living with her. They fought with each other all of the time. She kept saying that she wanted to change her life. Doug and I had offered to teach her the basic creating lessons. She made several appointments, but always had excuses and didn't come. After many months she finally showed up, and was taught the very basic principles. Something that is taught, don't believe what we tell you, experiment for yourself. That night, instead of being angry and yelling at her kids, she sent them love and blessings. The next morning her daughter, who she'd recently thrown out of the house, came back. Only this time, instead of yelling, she hugged her mother, told her she loved her, and told her she was doing a really good job, something she hadn't done before. There was no arguing or yelling. The neighbor was amazed. She said that she had never had such a nice atmosphere surrounding her, in her home. When she went to work, there was a letter from one of her customers, wishing her a good day and thanking her for being a thoughtful and helpful person. She managed to keep a smile on her face even when she had to deal with her landlord, who was a friend of her boss and came in the restaurant, and her boss who always gave her a hard time. She was amazed that what she learned had worked. Then she was ready to try for a new job and apartment. That day, her son kept promising to pick up a few newspapers so she could look for both, but he never did. That day, he brought her some newspapers. She made a list of apartments and went to see some of them. Also, a new job appeared. Only she was afraid she couldn't handle the good things and believed she didn't deserve to have them. Instead of embracing what she wanted, she made excuses and returned to her comfort zone, which was chaos. She didn't visit for awhile, and when she did, she had lost both the old and new jobs, and she hadn't been paying her rent so the land lord was trying to evict her.

She said she wanted change, but when it appeared, she got scared. She couldn't step beyond her comfort zone; she wasn't ready to deal with new choices.

When the mother of one of our students learned how to create her new job; she also wanted a new car. She understood what she had done for the job and was so excited she actually started programming her car. The results happened too fast for her comfort zone, and she pulled back. She said she couldn't handle the car that fast and she wanted more time. A few months later, she got her car.

Doug's family was Catholic. He was raised Catholic. He went to a Catholic High School. His family expected him to marry a nice Catholic girl. Apparently, all of his girlfriends before me were Catholic. They also believed all people in their lives should have blond hair. (They were also all blond, except his mother who was a redhead.) When he brought me into their lives, and worse, when he told them he was marrying me (I was not Catholic and I had black hair.), they had a really hard time. Doug's marrying me really upset their belief systems and pushed the limits of their comfort zones.

You create through the eyes with which you view the world. You create from your comfort zone.

Keeping Your Power

Your power is the energy field that surrounds you, and is you. It is the vibration you send out to the universe, and the vibration you receive back. It acts like an antenna, calling the like things into your life. Fear is giving away your power. Anger is giving away your power. Everyone wants to be loved, and you will go to extraordinary measures to fulfill that desire. Love is the signal everyone wants to send out and receive back. What you need to understand, is that you have, to have a healthy love and respect for yourself first, before you know how to accept and give love to others. All the things you've learned and accepted about yourself over the years are the patterns you accept for your creations. They are your expectations and practiced responses.

You have to understand that you make your own happiness; so, if you are happy with who you are, you will draw things and situations that will keep you in that happy frame of mind. If you except something from someone and it doesn't work out the way you think it should, does it mean that you need to understand, or that you are the one who holds the power to make yourself happy? Keep your power.

There is a story about keeping your power from a tool I call the "Buddha gift." Buddha would be out doing his thing, and this guy comes along and calls Buddha a hypocrite, a liar, a bum, the scum of the earth, and all kinds of other names. Buddha smiled, and continued on his way as if nothing happened. The next day, Buddha met the same man. The man called Buddha all of those things again, and worse. Again, Buddha smiled and continued on his way as if nothing happened. This same thing happened several days in a row. Buddha's calm reaction to what the man did only upset the man more and more until one day, the man said, "Buddha, I torment you day after day and it never affects you. You stay calm and happy while I just become more upset. How can this be?" The Buddha answered, "If someone gives you a gift and you don't accept it, who has the gift?"

If someone gives you a pile of crap and you don't accept it, what happens? The person who offered the crap knows he still has it. He now has to get rid of it at all costs. He has accepted it in his realm, and try as he might, can't get rid of it. It has upset his whole being.

My husband taught this practice in a much more poignant way. He explained it this way: If someone gives you a gift of shit, what happens? You reach out and accept it. First, it is on your hands. You look at it. It looks like shit. You bring it up to your nose. It smells like shit. But now, it's all over your face and in your mouth. You can't get rid of it fast enough. You shake your hands, some of it falls down on the ground; you move and step on it. It's on your shoes and you are totally immersed in it. If you refuse the gift, who has it? This, in essence, is giving your power away.

While I was looking through my journals for stories about giving up your power and telling myself my brain was processing the information, I had to deal with pieces of my belief system and the understanding of keeping my power; in my head, I am a writer, I have always been a writer. When I was a kid, I helped pass the time by writing poetry in the margins of my notebooks. I was thrilled with writing poetry, because I could see finished results really fast. I did that all through high school and college. It never occurred to me to expand my writing I most likely didn't think I could.

My favorite style was the Rod McKuen style, which was very lyrical. When I was dating Doug, I finally got bold enough to show him some of my writing. He read it over and said that the poems were all right but he would rather have his poems rhyme. I tried a few rhyming poems, and found them stupid, so I gave up writing. But in my head, I was a writer, and as I studied and read, I learned about journal writing and would do that from time to time. I kept detailed accounts of my thoughts, feelings, and life. Several times when I was really into my journal writing, Doug told me he liked that I was writing, but then told me he thought I was wasting my time just journal writing and I would give up writing again for a while. But in my head, I'm a write. So, eventually, I'd go back to writing, even if it was just journal writing.

When I was talking to two of my friends about writing this chapter, one of them asked me what it meant to give up your power. I told her a story about something the other one had said to me. Years ago I started another book, which also I haven't finished, I showed the woman the first chapter and it had examples of learning how to be joyful through the eyes of children and animals. She asked me, "What if the person reading the book doesn't like children or animals?" At that point, I put the book away. I said to the woman asking the question that's giving your power away; not believing in yourself.

When I was a little girl I liked to sing. I would sing all the time. Then one day, my father told me I had a voice that sounded like a fog horn, and I quit singing. As I grew up, I often found myself in places where I had to sing in a group. I sang because I had to, and when the teacher came near, I would I would lip sync. I did this in high school and college. Since everyone else in class had to sing at the same time, I felt safe. In college, it was a choral conducting class. The teacher also taught our sight singing and ear training class; he was an assistant director for the lyric opera. That man knew voices. So, when he came near our section, I would definitely lip sync. Then for my sight singing exam, I had to sing the intervals and whatever for him by myself. I did what I was supposed to do, and he told me I had a voice that was crystal clear and pleasing, and he wished I would sing louder in class. That was a long way from fog horn to crystal clear and pleasing. But the old belief was difficult to give up; it was much safer to hide behind the "fog horn." Even later, in our own band, I took voice lessons. In high school chorus, I was a tenor, the "fog horn" theory; also, we didn't have very many tenors, so I got designated. In college, I did the second alto, so later, when I went to the voice teacher, she took me through exercises to find out my range. She said who ever told me I was alto was wrong, and instead, I was a second soprano. She got notes out of me I never dreamed of hitting by myself. Even after all of that, it was safer to hide behind the "fog horn" theory.

"Sticks and Stones will break my bones but names will never hurt me." Be careful what you let in your realm. Don't put so many things in your path that you're afraid of what you most want and cancel it out; keep your power. TV commercials, friends, family everything around you influence your choices. You have to learn how to make the choices you want without accepting other influences.

Our society teaches you to feel sorry for victims. Everyone jumps up and down defending the right to be a victim, and are perfectly comfortable blaming someone else for your circumstances. It is really hard to except the responsibility for some of the choices you've allowed in your life. First of all, give yourself credit for whatever you have created. Whatever you created, you have to admit it's really amazing. When you understand and accept that you created it, you will understand that you can change it. And, if you understand, and accept you created, it you will have learned that particular lesson that you have set up for yourself.

When you don't like what you've created, change the way you look at it. All the choices are yours. You are in charge. Keep your power.

"Tools"

The past few chapters showed some of the "tools" in action. Now here is a list of some other "tools." I hope this list helps with your creating:

1. Understand your realm.
2. There is a purpose to all you select to do.
3. Watch your like things and synchronicity.
4. Follow the easiest path.
8. Make a statement. It is one of the most powerful things you can do. Words bring reality. Every type of verbalization creates a vibration and vibration creates form.
9. Making statements about thoughts or beliefs make physical things happen.
10. Make your thoughts and statements in the present. I am rich, as opposed to, I want to be rich, or I am getting rich. Getting is never having.
11. Listen to what you say.
12. When you ask, you already have it.
13. Create a Mantra, which would be your affirmations.
14. When you pray. Say thank-you as if you already have what you want, instead of me asking for everything. And act as if you already have what you want.
15. When an opportunity arises, take advantage of it. Be prepared to just do it

16. Understand your track record, dealing with how you deal with what you want.
17. Frustration when it appears, means that you have to look at what is making your emotional level go up, and what conflict there is in your thoughts; and change how you look at the situation.
18. If you hear people make comments that are not part of their normal speech patterns, pay attention to this. It is a message from spirit about what you are creating.
19. Expectation. Expect what you want to happen, to happen. Think of it as already done. Make sure to say Thank-you. Accept it as already done.
20. Make a list. Check your list. If nothing is happening ask yourself why? And what are you doing about it?
21. If you don't see things happening, through the straight forward, front way, check other directions that aren't so obvious. Shift your focus, side step, this is called "the backdoor approach."
22. At what point in time, will you allow what it is, you want to happen.
23. Watch your body language and the body language of the people around you.
24. Consider whatever you are doing as a done deal, already handled.
25. Have fun. Laugh and be happy. Don't think like a human; ridiculous, no logic.
26. View your creations with the wonderment of a child.
27. Never stop trying.
28. Create from no Ego.
29. As you approach life, answers will be given to you.
30. Send blessings.
31. Attachment, don't become too attached to things.
32. Use: wish, desire, exception, and passion.
33. Create from peace in body, thought, and feeling.
34. When you don't like something, change how you feel about it.
35. Have compassion.
36. Acknowledge all that is.
37. Create from being nonjudgmental.

38. Live in the now: no "I should of's," or "I could of's," or "I would but's."
39. Keep your power.
40. What is the menu for today? Plan your day.
41. Who says?
42. There is no problem, that can't be solved by the conciseness that created it.
43. All consciousness is connected.
44. Don't trust or believe anyone.
45. Take responsibility for the journey.
46. Trust spirit.

When you want to create something, do you put your order in and don't worry about it, or do you put your order in and keep checking and altering it? It's like when you cloud the "I want the piece of carrot cake," with flipping the emotion switch, everything that you have ever thought said or done turns your easy creation into chaos. Now you attract all the synchronicities of how it will be so difficult to get the piece of carrot cake, your process might be, "I want a piece of carrot cake, but it is not good for me." It will make me gain weight. Oh, but it would taste so good. Oh, it will be so much work to fix it. I don't have the time to prepare it. It is only something I get on special occasions. So it doesn't appear to happen for you right away. You let you emotions get in the way. When the process should be that you know exactly what you want. I want a piece of carrot cake. Visualize it as clearly as possible. Taste it. Smell it. And let it go. Trust the universe and you will have your piece of carrot cake.

When you don't like something, change the way you look at it. It is like the word two. If someone asks you to spell the word two you could get the answers t w o, t o and t o o. There are several different ways of looking at the same thing. Everyone's realm is different. The signals you are sending out are the realities you get back; multilayered and multi-dimensional.

Pebbles in the Water

I have been working on this book for several years. Most of the people who were all excited about it have long given up on me. Others though look forward to each new chapter and each revision. It has been written like an open water faucet; while the water was turned on, the pages come rushing forth on full blast, but when the water is shut off, nothing. No matter what I say or do about it though, I always wind up back here, working on the book. It has a mind and life of its own; again, multilayered and multi-dimensional. It was meant to be completed, but never finished.

When I first started this book, my son said this should be the first chapter because he liked the title. For most of the writing, a chapter with this title has just been set in the back ground containing notes if they were ever needed. But I think it is a great title for the concluding chapter. Each one's life journey is like water and in constant motion. You create your own reality. You are all on uniquely different paths. You have all chosen your own lessons.

All consciousness is connected. Everything you have ever thought, said, or done, makes up whom you are, and who you, will become. Not only does that affect you but like throwing a pebble in the water, the rings spread out indefinitely; everything you have ever thought, said, or done, spreads out to affect so many others. You are not just the person you see in the mirror. Each person is a: baby, a child, a teenager, a young adult, an older adult, an old person, a daughter, a sister, a wife, a mother, a grandmother, or a son, a brother a husband, a father, a grandfather. Each person is more than just one thing, and that's only on the physical level. You choose your experiences and how you experience them, and what you learn and bring away from them. Multi-layered has several things happening at the same time. You don't stop where the ends of your physical body stops, you are part of all consciousness. Multi-dimensional; many things happening on different levels. Your life is constantly expanding, moving, and changing, whether it seems to be or not; nothing stands still. You are constantly creating.

Although all conscience is connected, each of you makes up your own lives. What you experience in your life, the people around you don't experience what you are experiencing in the same way. If I ask you to spell the word "2"; no explanation is necessary. Some of you might spell it "to," others could spell it "too," and still others could spell it "two." They are all correct spellings of "2".

My father's favorite joke was, "How do you get down off an elephant?"

Answer, "You don't. You get down off a duck."

He told that joke constantly when I was young, and I had no understanding of that type of down. Like so many other people he told the joke to, I only understood physical climbing; so for a long time, I didn't understand the joke.

When I was ten years-old, and was taking organ lessons, I was asked to perform in the church Christmas program. I was to play four Christmas Carols during the offertory. I had to play on the church organ, which was bigger and more complicated than mine. I practiced the songs, which were no problem, and I rehearsed how to change the sounds for each song. Before the offertory, I had my music set up, and the piece of paper that told me which buttons to press to change the sounds in-between songs. When it was time to perform, I went up there and started playing the songs. The first two went really well; then, just before going into the third song, the piece of paper with my directions for sound changes blew off the organ, and on to the floor. I panicked, but only in my head. I continued playing, and, when I went into the third song, I pushed the button. It was the wrong button and made a different sound than I was expecting. It sounded harsher. I thought I ruined the whole thing. I pushed the button with the original sound, and finished the last two songs. I finished my performance and ran to my seat crying. I cried and cried and no one could figure why I was upset. I was told over and over that I did really well, and in their eyes, that was true. What they saw was a little girl who could play the Christmas carols well, and brave enough to get up there and perform. What I saw was me having messed up. The reality was different for all of us; "two", "to", "too".

So we draw to the end of the book. I hope you enjoyed it and that you have a better understanding; you create your life, and now have some ways to consciously create things in your life.

When you create something for yourself that you are amazed with, it is like trying to explain a beautiful sunset. You can try to describe it, but unless you experience it yourself, you don't understand the real feeling.

Have fun creating . . . Love, blessings and peace.